SAINT AELRED OF RIEVAULX

To be without a friend is loneliness indeed! But what happiness, what security and joy to have someone with whom to speak confidently, as with another self, with whom to share all one's failures and success, and who can be trusted with the deeper secrets of one's heart.

Aelred of Rievaulx

SAINT AELRED OF RIEVAULX

Paul Diemer OCSO

Gracewing.

This edition first published in 1997

Gracewing
Fowler Wright Books
2 Southern Avenue
Leominster
Herefordshire HR6 0QF

ISBN 0 85244 451 6

Typesetting by
Action Typesetting Limited, Gloucester GL1 1SP

Printed by Cromwell Press
Broughton Gifford, Wiltshire SN12 8PH

Saint Aelred of Rievaulx

'How clearly the Gospel has come to life in them ... a happy race of men whose habit, whose diet, whose entire life savours of the Gospel! God alone is their portion, so that they abide in God and God in them. ... The Gospel seems as it were to live again in them.' This was how the group of Cistercian monks, who had founded the monastery of Rievaulx, appeared to some of the Benedictine community of St Mary's at York.

The Cistercians, known as White monks because of their habit made from undyed wool, were members of the Benedictine family; they belonged to a 'protest' group which just over thirty years earlier had founded the new monastery of Cîteaux in a solitude in Burgundy. They were protesting, not against the Rule of St Benedict, but against customs and interpretations which had grown up round the Rule since its composition in the sixth century, and had obscured its original directness and simplicity. Some of these customs were cultural; others, liturgical ones, had been introduced to suit contemporary devotion, while others were perhaps 'mitigations' of the austerities of the Rule, austerities that were there not for their own sake, but as means or tools to be used by men who belonged to a race which had, in some deeply mysterious way, once turned away from God, but were now trying to journey back to God in response to his call.

The Cistercian movement was not simply a negative criticism of the Black monk's way of life. It developed at a time when renewal was in the air, and the first Cistercians came from the Benedictine monastery of Molesme which had itself been founded not many years earlier by a group of hermits who were seeking a more fervent way of life. But Molesme in its maturity had lost something of its first inspiration.

The group who founded Cîteaux, under the leadership of Sts Robert, Alberic and Stephen Harding, also wanted solitude. Not precisely so that individuals could lead a hermit life, but solitude for the community as a whole, to provide an atmosphere of quietness and peace for prayer, away from the busyness of the ordinary life of the world. They also wanted a real poverty which united them to the poor Christ, and also to the poor of Christ whom they saw living around them. This desire for poverty was also inspired by the early Christian community as described by St Luke, where all things were held in common and there was a sharing among them according to the needs of each – a sharing which united them into a community having one heart and one mind.

In a spirit of unity they discussed their new way of life at Cîteaux. They simplified: modified their clothing, bedding and diet, and rejected customs that had grown up around the Rule of St Benedict. They made their structures minimal, as we would say today. They paid special attention to Chapter 73 of the Rule which looks beyond St Benedict to the Desert Fathers and the early monks of the Thebaid.

After ten years, an Englishman from Dorset, Stephen Harding, became their third abbot. He was a man of deep prayer and a lover of solitude, pleasant and homely in speech, cheerful, and liked by everyone. He had a great love of scripture and of beautiful books and manuscripts. In spite of their ascetic life and the hard work involved in clearing the ground, Cîteaux became under Stephen a unique centre of monastic culture. This small community out in the wilds initiated a liturgical reform, made a collection of what they believed to be the authentic hymns and gregorian melodies, brought out an edition of the Bible and composed a document for monastic government (later known as the Charter of Charity) which was full of wisdom and foresight. The four volumes of Stephen's Bible completed in 1109 (just eleven years after the foundation of Cîteaux) constitute one of the richest treasuries of contemporary French miniatures. Helped by professionals they finished a copy of Gregory's *Moralia* illustrated with little pictures of monks harvesting, weaving, gathering grapes, felling a tree and so on, a witness to the outstanding artistic gifts and culture of this small community.

Stephen was a man of inexhaustible charity and saw to it that the monastic purse was an open treasury to all in need. There was a famine and his own brethren were in need; there was no food and no money, and there were deaths in the community. We are told God visited them in two ways; first through Elizabeth de Vergy, described as one of the most attractive personalities of twelfth-century Burgundy. She gave, and inspired friends to give them farms, vineyards and meadows. Cîteaux was at the spiritual crossroads; would it be the story of Molesme all over again? But the monks re-affirmed their decision for renewal and took steps to safeguard their apartness from the world, their poverty and simplicity, even in regard to their church and their form of worship. So renewal became something that was built into Cistercianism.

Secondly, God visited them through vocations, with the

4

coming of St Bernard and his companions. Two or three years later Bernard was sent with a small group to found Clairvaux, and it was from Clairvaux in 1132 that he sent the men who were to establish Rievaulx. It was no haphazard venture; the matter was discussed with the English king, Henry I, and with the local Baron who donated the land, Walter Espec. As leader, Bernard chose William, his own secretary (later venerated as St William), who was himself an Englishman. These men brought to Ryedale the Cistercian life, with its two great characteristics of love of the Rule in all its simplicity, and love of solitude. It was just thirty-four years after the foundation of Cîteaux.

Aelred entered the novitiate of Rievaulx two years later in 1134, being about twenty-four years old. His father Eilaf had been the priest at Hexham and at one time treasurer of Durham. Eilaf, like his father and grandfather before him, was a married priest and belonged to an Anglo-Saxon family of old Northumbrian stock. They had lived through the devastation of the North by William the Conqueror, and survived the tensions caused by having Norman bishops intent on reform introduced at Durham. Eilaf himself was a learned, respectable and conscientious man, well known to the neighbouring king of Scotland; and King David's son Henry and his own boy Aelred grew up together at Hexham and at the royal court. Later the king made Aelred his seneschal or steward. It was a position of trust and responsibility and gives evidence not only of David's affection for the young man but also of Aelred's capabilities as a practical administrator. He had a clear head for the understanding of affairs and a gift for dealing with men; because of these qualities the king sent him on a matter of business to Thurstan, archbishop of York. While

he was in Yorkshire, he heard of the monks at Rievaulx and, having finished his business in York, he rode out to Walter Espec's castle at Helmsley where he spent the night. Walter, the founder of the abbey and one of King Henry I's leading barons, has been described as a huge man with a great black beard and a voice like a trumpet. He gave Aelred a great welcome and the next day took him to Rievaulx to meet the monks. This visit undoubtedly made a great impression on Aelred, but he returned at the end of the day with Walter to Helmsley. Early next morning he said goodbye to his host and set out on his journey home to Scotland. Their way took them along the top of the ridge overlooking the valley of the Rye (now beautifully laid out with lawns and known as Rievaulx terrace). The view across the valley is one of the most exquisite in England. But Aelred, looking down through the trees would have seen, not the lovely Gothic choir that is there today, nor even the severe Norman nave, but a cluster of temporary buildings set between the slopes of the hill and the fast-flowing stream. The peace of the setting, the simplicity of the monastery and above all the meaning of why it was there − a school of Christ, a school of the Lord's service − all this stirred Aelred to the depths. When they reached the narrow road that wound down the hill to the gatehouse he asked his companion if he would like to go down to the abbey again. Aelred later admitted that all had depended on the man's reply. It was yes. Aelred was stirred but he was not yet committed. The monks for their part questioned him, investigated his motives, and may even have used persuasion. But once he had made his decision he could hardly wait for the four days to pass before he would be admitted as a novice. After a year he made his profession according to the Rule of St Benedict.

His biographer, Walter David, a monk of the house and later Aelred's infirmarian, tells us that he was a cheerful hard-working member of the community. Though not strong, he was deft and practical, cool in a crisis, and did what he had to do without fuss. Above all he developed a taste for prayer. All this did not go unnoticed, and Abbot William made him a member of his council, discovering in him unsuspected depths of wisdom and prudence together with a gift for disentangling difficult cases. He was also a good speaker, knew what he wished to say and said it well. As a result he was sent by his abbot on a diplomatic mission to Rome in connexion with the appointment of the new archbishop of York. On his return he was made novice-master of the fast-growing community which already numbered 300. Also, at the request of Bernard, whom he had met at Clairvaux, he began to write his best-known work *The Mirror of Charity* which was a treatise on the place of love in the growth of man's personal relationship with God, and with his fellow-men.

After only a few months as novice-master he was appointed first abbot of Revesby in Lincolnshire – the third foundation of Rievaulx. Five years later in 1147 he was elected abbot of the house of his profession and returned to Rievaulx as its third abbot, a position he occupied until his death in 1167.

Aelred seems to have had a special charism for his ministry as abbot. But we must not forget that first and foremost he was a Cistercian monk who had vowed to seek God along the way traced out by the Rule of St Benedict. He had grasped the basic Christian teaching, which the Cistercians made especially their own, that we would not be seeking God unless we had already been found by Him; that God loved us first while we were still sinners, and actually gives the power to men to return love for love. Life was a journey and the end of the journey, whose whole meaning was love, was already there in germ at its beginning. Aelred, steeped as he was in the Scriptures, saw this journey, this monastic/Christian life in biblical terms. St Benedict was a second Moses, a leader taking his monks, the special people of God, out of the bondage of sin – out of the Egypt of this world – through the desert of life to the promised land of heaven and the city of Jerusalem, which was no longer simply the vision of peace, but the vision of God himself. Christ had gone on before; St Benedict followed with his monks on this journey back to the Father. Christ himself was also the way. The monk followed this way by committing himself to Christ in faith, a faith that was not simply an act of the mind, but a surrender in absolute dependence to the care of God; a surrender which was truly radical because it reached to the roots of a man's being where he is most alone and most in need of security. This faith was expressed by a commitment of love to the person of Christ and by a merciful, compassionate bearing love towards one's brothers. It was a love that would find its full flowering in the face-to-face vision of Christ who would be fully recognized as the perfect revelation of the Godhead.

The way was Christ, but it was also the narrow way of his Gospel teaching, which, as St Benedict pointed out, was, especially at the beginning, a hard and rugged way. It could not be otherwise, for Christ's way was the way of the Cross which was the complete contradiction of the comfortable way of life. 'Our way of life is the Cross of Christ,' said Aelred. He meant that the monastic way with its worship, vigils, abstinence, doing the will of another, bearing patiently one another's weaknesses, was the way

by which a monk carried not simply his own cross but shared in the Cross of Christ; and was inserted, as it were, into the saving act of Calvary which redeemed the world. He did not use the phrase 'Paschal Mystery' but he was speaking of the working out of the Paschal Mystery – the Passion, Death and Resurrection of Christ in our daily lives, just as his fellow-countryman Langland was to do two centuries later.

But all this could not be done on one's own: Aelred taught that just as the Jews needed Moses as their mediator, so monks needed Benedict. He is more than a mediator, rather a Father who has begotten us in Christ, and who obtains for us by his mediation the grace and spiritual power to put his teaching, which is simply that of the Gospel, into practice. Aelred points out that as a father Benedict has transmitted life to his sons, the life which he himself had received from above, so that as his monks grow in monastic virtues and in prayer, so too they grow in the likeness of Christ.

To live the teaching of the Gospel is certainly not the prerogative of monks. It is the ideal of every Christian. It is simply that there are different ways of doing this. All are called to holiness – to union with God; from every vocation in life there is a doorway leading to the heart of God; so, for instance, the parent who accepts his life and gives his life as a parent, grows and becomes holy as a parent and his parenthood will give him an insight into the ways of God who is the Father of all.

The monk is called to a rather special way of life, which is his form of Christian living; his maturity and identity will depend on how he lives this life in its fulness. When we look at this life in detail as it was lived at Rievaulx and other Cistercian abbeys in England, we see that it fell into

three main areas: work, reading and prayer. These were not three separate compartments in a monk's day. It is true that there were specific times for each of these activities, but they blended together to form an integral whole. The thoughts gained from a monk's reading carried over into his prayer and his work; the fruits of his prayer affected his work and his dealings with others; and work done conscientiously in silence could lead to compunction or contemplation in prayer.

The Cistercians wanted to earn their own living, to be self-supporting and have something over to give to the poor. The labour for this was to come from the monks, lay brothers and hired workers. Lay brothers had been introduced in the very early years at Cîteaux, when the monks found it almost impossible to give the required amount of time to the services in choir and reading, and also spend sufficient time on the land, especially when their fields were at some distance from the monastery. So they introduced lay brothers, men under vows like themselves but who were given a form of prayer that was simpler than the Office in choir. Once trained, they were skilled and competent in helping to build, develop and maintain a Cistercian abbey, and many were men of deep contemplative prayer. The Cistercians were not the first to think of the idea of a lay brotherhood, but they were the first to develop it on such a scale; it is a good example of how they were prepared to innovate in order to keep not simply the letter of the Rule but also its spirit. The lay-brother vocation opened the monastic life to many for whom it would otherwise have been closed; when Aelred was abbot, there were between four and five hundred lay brothers at Rievaulx, and on Sundays and great feasts when they came in from the granges they filled the Church 'like bees

packed in a hive'.

Serfs – almost the equivalent of slaves – were forbidden, as were ecclesiastical revenues, likewise the system by which mills were owned and run as a source of income. Gradually, however, serfs began to be acquired either by purchase or by gift with grants of land that included the serfs living there. And as early as 1157 the General Chapter at Cîteaux had to make legislation regarding the evasion of rules concerning mills, and later issued prohibitions against the possession of churches with their incomes, a practice which was involving the monasteries in lawsuits and rivalries. Gradually the changing economy of the surrounding countryside had its effect on the White monks – the disappearance of the serf class and the rise of the small farmers lessened the number of vocations to the lay brothers, but though they did the same kind of things as any other monastic group of the time, it might be argued that the Cistercian economy always remained less complicated than in some of the Black-monk houses.

Primarily the Cistercians were farmers; in England the cultivation of grain crops was normal and basic to their system. But some houses like Sawley and Jervaulx were situated in cold, damp districts where the crops would not ripen, so such houses developed their livestock. Rievaulx had horses and in the twelfth century received a single pasture for sixty mares with their foals – Dieulacre had at least seventy mares – but Jervaulx was most famous of all for the quality of its horses; a reputation which was maintained right down to the Reformation, and even some twentieth-century bloodstock goes back to the Jervaulx line. Pig-farming was another Cistercian activity; the outlay was cheap and the returns good, especially where the monastery had access to woods with acorns and nuts;

the pig meat was sold, while the grease was invaluable for the softening and waterproofing of leather boots.

But it is as sheep farmers that the great Cistercian abbeys of the North are best known. Their situation near moorlands and wolds with large areas for free-range grazing, their system of granges run by lay brothers, all helped to make sheep farming with its annual wool crop a profitable enterprise. It was largely through their work that their high quality wool crop became one of the assets of the country and the abbey of Fountains an important clearing centre. Cistercian abbeys were usually built near a river and the monks were skilful in diverting water for all necessary domestic purposes. Rivers were valuable too for fishing, as sources of power for mills, and also for transport. Tintern had its own harbour on the river Wye and Furness and Holmcultram both owned ships – presumably for buying grain from Ireland. Netley and Beaulieu had them too, and sent grain to France and brought back wine and other provisions. Sometimes abbeys were close to areas of mineral deposit and these resources were soon exploited. Rievaulx, Kirkstead, Sawley and Byland were running iron furnaces from the twelfth century – but the greatest producer was Furness which had forty in operation in the thirteenth century. Salt, so necessary for preserving food, was produced at many abbeys; Newminster and others had salt works quite early in their history.

There were probably other smaller industries as well and we get a hint from Aelred's letter to his sister that flax was grown and made into linen at Rievaulx. (Structural evidence in the oldest part of the ruins would suggest that there was also a tannery in Aelred's time.) As a practical administrator ultimately responsible for the temporal as well as the spiritual welfare of his monastery, Aelred was interested in all that was going on around him, and in his sermons and treatises often used illustrations which would be familiar in the day-to-day life of his monks and brothers. The work at Rievaulx was heavy and demanding; as a novice he sometimes fell asleep over his reading from sheer weariness.

Reading was another important area in the life of a Cistercian, the *lectio divina* of Benedict's Rule, holy because its aim and purpose was to lead the reader to a deeper communion with God. Holy also, because most of a monk's reading came from Holy Scripture and commentaries on the sacred text. It was a slow meditative reading which sought not simply information for the mind, but rather the formation of the whole person to the likeness of Christ; not simply knowledge about God, but that loving knowledge of him as a person which the Bible describes in terms of the union between husband and wife. Aelred taught that the monk was not simply reading about God's dealings with men in the past, and events in Christ's life that were over and done with. Rather, by prayerfully reflecting upon and 'ruminating' what he was reading, the monk was brought into contact with that same God, present now in his soul. He could enter by faith and love into these same mysteries of Christ's life on earth, and make his own in 'the here and now' the special graces offered by each mystery, by each saving event.

This remembrance, this *memoria*, which made God present in a new and life-giving way, was the monastic way of reflecting on the message of revelation, the monastic way of doing theology. It differed from the more speculative and analytical methods of the later 'schools' – methods which could be independent of the moral and spiritual life of the student, and which were based more on philosophy and metaphysics than on Scripture and the writings of the Fathers. For the monastic method, asceticism, humility and prayer, which led to purity of heart, were needed to prepare the way for this contact with the living God; and so it might be called a kind of 'living theology'. It was a theology often expressed in terms of symbols, parables and allegories, but its best exponents like Bernard and Aelred never allowed it to remain in the realm of the symbol. It had to be linked with reality and applied to the individual; just as the prophet Nathan, after recounting his parable, could point to King David and say: 'You are the man.'

In his *Letter to his Sister* and the little treatise *On Jesus at Twelve Years Old* Aelred suggests the same way of meditation – inserting oneself into the Gospel – as Bernard did in his Rule for the Knights Templar; a way that St Ignatius was to develop, perhaps as a result of reading the life of Christ by Ludolph of Saxony. And it has been suggested that Ludolph himself was influenced by the meditations of Aelred. Today, as men of our time, we cannot ignore the 800 years of development in methods of study, and new scientific ways of thinking which separate us from Aelred. But even so, Aelred and his contemporaries have much to teach us about the way our reading should not only inform, but form us. Perhaps their method should complete and fulfil our modern ways of reflecting on the Christian mysteries.

The third area of a monk's life, one that should permeate the rest of it, was that of prayer. The Divine Office, the work of God to which Benedict said nothing should be preferred, formed a back ground for personal prayer. Verses from the psalms and readings would come to mind during the day and these the monk could make his own; and Aelred's sermons are full of little phrases from the Office. He was very conscious of the way the Office was performed in his Abbey, and once remarked that visiting Abbots were checking the weight of the portions of bread in the refectory whilst missing the fervour with which the Office was being sung in choir. He had strong views about the way monks should sing. 'What are we doing,' he writes, 'with the thunder of organ music, the clash of cymbals and elaborate part-settings for different voices? We hear monks doing all sorts of ridiculous things with their voices, plaguing us with womanish falsettos, spavined bleatings and tremulos. I have even seen them waving their arms about, beating time to the music and contracting their bodies in all directions ... and the mere sound of singing is preferred to the meaning of the words that are sung. Sense and sound together are meant to stir us to devotion, and so the sound of our music must be sober and moderate ... and not trespass on the words so that our minds are distracted from their meaning.'

He was also in the Cistercian tradition when he wrote that 'the man who has found Jesus' company within his own soul ... is happy enough to say his prayers in a little chapel of rough unpolished stone where there is nothing carved or painted to distract the eye, no fine hangings, no marble pavements, no blaze of candles, no glittering of golden vessels'.

The point of this simplicity was to remove distractions which could stimulate the imagination instead of quietening it, in preparation for the quiet, almost wordless, prayer of the heart, a form of prayer that goes back beyond the Rule to the early monks of Mount Sinai. It is the prayer of centring – a prayer that is as old as the hills. It is for this kind of prayer that monks need leisure, in the sense of being free from business. It means being empty, disengaged, free, not tied down by created things, so that one is available for God. It means entering into the 'rest of the Sabbath'. It is no idle rest, for, as Aelred explains, it is filled

with a contemplative gazing on the Lord. It is this gazing, this being with Him, that gives us a share in his peace and in his dynamic rest, because it unites us with Him.

Words like 'leisure', being 'empty', 'idle' or 'at rest', have a rather negative sound for us today, but the content of the leisure was a very positive making-oneself-available for God so as to be capable of enjoying Him; and in its wider sense this covered the whole meaning of the monastic way of life. Apartness from the world, asceticism, meditation on the Word that was life, all this orientated the life of a Cistercian towards contemplation. It was the response to a call that could only reach its fulfilment in Heaven, when our longing would no longer be bound by the limitations of the flesh and we should see Jesus Christ as God. Being drawn into his glorious light and lost in his unbelievable joy, this will be the Sabbath of Sabbaths, when we return to our Maker to whom we belong, and who is Himself our greatest possession. We shall have received the Holy Spirit with the very perfection and fulfilment of all He can give, and with Him the outpouring of that love beside which servile fear is no more. This is the Sabbath of Sabbaths – the goal of St Benedict's Rule – and from what his biographer tells us, Aelred had at least a foretaste of this towards the end of his life as he prayed in his little oratory. The monastic life with its call to a close union with God is basically a contemplative life. But it seems that the invitation to the mystical life was preached in Cistercian houses in a way that was not to be found in other monastic reforms of the time.

In 1147 Aelred was elected abbot by the community at Rievaulx. Not far away at Byland Roger was abbot, while Fountains was in the care of Henry Murdac. Both these men were friends of Aelred – Roger, twenty years later, gave him the last sacraments and was present when he died. He had been sent from Furness, a Savigniac house, in 1134 as one of the group to make a foundation at Calder. This new monastery was destroyed by the Scots, so the community returned to Furness for shelter, where however they were unwelcome and were sent off again. Their wanderings were manifold; they moved to Old Byland, where they were so close to Rievaulx that the bells of the two monasteries caused confusion, then again to Stocking and finally to a site near Cuxwold. Roger, like Aelred, had great sympathy for the young, understanding their weaknesses and hesitations as well as their ideals and generosity. Aelred was called on to arbitrate in a dispute about jurisdiction over Byland. He decided in favour of Savigny.

Also in 1147 Henry Murdac, abbot of Fountains, became archbishop of York. His dissimilarity in character to Aelred did not prevent the two men becoming friends. Henry, sent to Fountains by Bernard, brought with him the full Cistercian observance in all its austerity. The community rose to the challenge with enthusiasm. But Henry was a stern man and so unafraid to speak his mind that once the citizens of York went out to Fountains intent on destroying the monastery and killing the abbot. They did indeed set fire to the church, but overlooked Henry lying prostrate before the altar. Often he was involved in controversy. He acted from a deep sense of duty and conscience; though intransigent, he was basically humble. As archbishop he retained a constant interest in his monastery, where he was succeeded as abbot by two of Aelred's monks from Rievaulx in succession. Aelred regarded Henry as a saint and kept for many years a cross which had belonged to him.

Aelred's contacts were not limited to neighbouring abbots

and members of his own Order. Walter Daniel tells us that he wrote letters to the pope, to the kings of England, France and Scotland, to most of the bishops and many of the great men of England. It is tantalizing to find just references to these letters, which survived at both Rievaulx and Margam in the later Middle Ages. Their loss is particularly disappointing because Walter Daniel commented that in them are to be found the spirit and the living image of Aelred.

Gradually he became a man of considerable influence, specially but not exclusively in the North of England. He had to make regular journeys on visitations to the daughter houses of Rievaulx, two of which, Melrose and Dundrennan, were in Scotland. He was also called in often as an adviser in disputes of various kinds. His great common sense, his flair for penetrating to the crux of the dispute, together with his obvious sincerity and the way he expressed his decisions, made him specially acceptable as an arbitrator. By nature he was a peacemaker, but remained always a man of his time, taking for granted that twelfth-century justice required harsh penalties.

He was well known to King Henry II, whom he persuaded to support Alexander III against the anti-pope Octavian. He was also a friend of the earl of Leicester, who became justiciar of England, and of Gilbert Foliot, bishop of London and critic of Thomas Becket.

One of the first acts of Alexander III after his recognition by Henry II was to canonize King Edward the Confessor. At the request of his kinsman Laurence, abbot of Westminster, Aelred rewrote the *Life of the Confessor* by Osbert of Clare. This became widespread and popular. He also wrote a homily on the new saint which he preached at Westminster Abbey when the relics of St Edward were translated in 1163, a ceremony presided over by the new archbishop of Canterbury, Thomas Becket. It was an event which gave Aelred great pleasure because an Anglo-Saxon king was being venerated for his holiness in the presence of a descendant of the Norman conqueror.

Aelred had dedicated to this descendant, now Henry II, his work *The Genealogy of the Kings of England*. For Henry was not only of Norman descent, but through his grandmother (the daughter of the justly famous queen, St Margaret of Scotland) he was related to Edmund Ironside and the old Anglo-Saxon kings of England. Thus he was a sorely-needed centre of unity for the country after the troubled reign of Stephen. Those fifteen years, the time of the Cistercian implantation in England, had seen the civil war with Matilda and the lawlessness of the Barons. They had been full of violence, terrorism and hardship for some monks as well as for ordinary people; in some parts of the country fighting and devastation were followed by famine.

At the accession of Henry II all looked forward to a return to normality; a period of enthusiastic expansion and monastic building began, which however was to lead many monasteries into debt. In the next century when the lovely Gothic choir was built, even Rievaulx suffered in this way.

Aelred was interested in history as part of his humanistic outlook, but it was particularly the people of the past rather than events which interested him. He wrote of St Cuthbert for whom he had a deep personal devotion, always committing himself to his safe-keeping while on his journeys. He wrote of the saints of his native Hexham and, in his treatise on the Battle of the Standard, of his friends who were fighting on opposite sides. Yet surprisingly, it must be admitted that these writings often lack the verve, vivid detail and pungent phrase of the old chroniclers, such as Jocelyn of Furness in his life of Aelred's friend, St Waltheof.

However, Aelred's real greatness lay especially in the kind of man he was, the kind of person he became. For one can sense a growth, a transformation over the years. The young man who entered Rievaulx was handsome, debonair, with an attractive friendly personality, a good mixer who could enjoy the company both of monks and of Walter Espec with his friends at Helmsley castle. He was not strong physically, and as the years passed he suffered intensely from gallstones; to this was added the agonies of arthritis, which at times were so great that he had to be carried by four men holding the corners of a linen sheet, and a mere touch would make him cry out in pain. The General Chapter gave him permission to live in the infirmary and to attend choir and Mass just when he was able. He was also left perfectly free to attend to the business of the house, the estate and its granges in the way he thought best and according to his health.

About ten years before his death he decided to have a little cell built near the infirmary where the brethren could visit him. This they did, twenty or thirty at a time, walking about the room, sitting on his bed, talking together, and Aelred would say: 'My sons, say what you like – only let there be no unseemly word, no detraction, no blasphemy.'

In this cottage, with its little oratory where he spent much time when he was well enough, he did most of his writing. Here he composed his treatises, his sermons and his letters.

About four years before his death he underwent a second conversion; he increased his austerities – dropping, not superfluities for he had none, but even things that were necessary for him in his weakness. He spent more time in prayer and vigils; and shut away in his little oratory often forgot all about the times for his meals. He gave more time

25

also to reading and he returned to the books which had been his guide and inspiration when he first left the world, especially the *Confessions* of St Augustine. It was as if he had had some fresh insight regarding his commitment to Christ, which resulted in a renewal of his desire to give himself utterly; this found expression in greater self-denial and a deepening of his life of prayer. This renewed presence of the Holy Spirit, if we may call it that, this fresh impulse of the life of Christ in his soul, showed itself especially in the gifts of prophecy and discernment of spirit that he received, and which were experienced by the community in his day-to-day dealings with them, and in his comments in Chapter. But also there was a renewal, as it were, in his personality which could be felt and recognized by others, even though it was difficult to put into words.

He was now living out the doctrine which he had begun to write about so many years before in his *Mirror of Charity*. He saw the monk as a true Christian, whose baptismal consecration was deepened and enabled to flower by monastic profession. It was no accident that the exodus theme was at the heart of his spirituality, because it was also the theme of Christ's life. Benedict was his leader, but only because he was following in the footsteps of Christ. There was no dichotomy between the monastic life and the Christian life, and all the monastic observances were geared to the following of Christ which was the only thing that mattered. It was a journey, like that of the Israelites through the desert; there were long periods of aridity and dryness, but there were oases too. The desert was a place where the monk struggled with temptations, but it was also a place where he encountered the Holy Spirit. Drawn further and further away from Egypt and its security, he was taught to depend on God alone – on the water which He provided in situations where it could be least expected – on the strength which came from the manna given day by day and which could not be collected and stored. It was a perfect allegory of the monastic/Christian life with its times of dryness and weariness, when there was the temptation to grumble and murmur, to make idols of work, study or something other than God who so often made Himself felt by His seeming absence. But there were times also when the monk came to an oasis and felt he was being cared for and carried by God as a man carried his little son with his cheek close against the child, or like an eagle leaving her nest and teaching her young to fly and catching them on her wings. If he was invited to enter the promised land, to seek a closer union with the Lord, he had to be courageous and trusting, ready to go forward into the unknown – unlike those Israelites who remained in their tents and sulked, afraid, refusing to put themselves into the hands of the God who had done so much for them. All this demanded not only faith but love. Aelred like other Cistercians of his time saw the true monk/Christian as a lover, as a person whose capacity to love was completely fulfilled, both with the commitment-love for God, and the merciful-compassionate love for others. He tells his sister (for the journey was the same for women as for men) to bind all the world into her heart with a bond of love and pity; her heart had to be a kind of Noah's ark in which there was room for everyone with their needs.

Like Julian of Norwich two hundred years later, Aelred saw that the meaning of the Christian life was love, love for God, for oneself and for one's fellow men. Love was not something sentimental or emotional, which resided only in the feelings and could change with the weather. It also had to do with the will and with the powers of reasoning. There could be a good love and a bad love – one that led from created things and swept upwards to God, and one that was selfish, possessive and turned away from God.

Like his master Augustine he saw that there were three human acts involved in love. Firstly there was the choice of what was to be loved and this involved a judgement of the mind, because sometimes our feelings could deceive us. We had to avoid choosing something that would lead us away from God, or something that was not for us because of our particular vocation in life. Choice was at the beginning of love, whether it was good or bad love. It was by his choices, by saying Yes or No, that a man became mature. But usually such choices were not made simply by cold reflection, for one's desires, needs, and feelings were involved as well. Then secondly the will had to move the person to act more positively to attain what was loved. Finally it rested in the possession and enjoyment of the object loved. The process was really a collaboration between reason, feelings and will, for it had to do with the whole person. Everyday experience showed that there were temptations to selfishness, and strong emotions could sway the whole personality; so there was need not only of God's help of guidance and discernment, but also of his creative power to carry out a right decision once it had been discerned.

True love, which is the charity spoken of in the New Testament, means that we have chosen something that is permitted for us in our particular way of life, that we have set about attaining it in the right way, and that we enjoy it in the way God intended and meant it to be enjoyed without grabbing or greed. It implies a complete turning away from sin, but leads to the true human happiness and peace of soul that come with a clean conscience. Charity is the soul's true Sabbath – the day on which it enters into the rest and enjoyment of God.

Love has to do not only with God, but also with ourselves and other people, Knowing and loving others, taking joy and delight in them is what we call friendship. Aelred himself tells us that as a boy he wanted only to love and to be loved. It was a trait that remained with him all his life for he was a man who was born for friendship; finally in his full maturity, about seven years before he died, he wrote a treatise on spiritual friendship. As a boy and a young monk he had read Cicero's book on friendship and it made a deep impression on him. His own treatise follows Cicero in that it takes the form of a dialogue, and this enables him to express the fruit of his experience in a personal, intimate and informal way; but his characters are much more vivid than those of Cicero; we feel they are real people carrying on a real discussion, and Walter Daniel especially comes alive. Aelred is not looking at friendship from the purely human point of view, he is more concerned with its spiritual benefits, and so, much of his teaching and examples are taken from the Fathers and from Scripture. He takes examples of all types of friendships from the Old Testament; and uses the Wisdom books to discuss the qualities of friends, how one should choose them, and how one should develop the different types of friendship – for all friendship is not on the same level. But it is in the New Testament that he finds the supreme example of friendship in Jesus himself who gave the uttermost proof of his love by laying down his life for his friends, and by giving himself to them, to be assimilated into their very substance, in the Eucharist.

It was union with Jesus that he saw as the basis of all

Christian friendship, and he found it exemplified in the early Church where the believers were the followers of Christ and shared in the breaking of the Bread, the prayers and the joy of the Holy Spirit, and had but one heart and one mind. True friendship must be founded on virtue, he said, for friendship is a form of love and love is of God. It does not exist to satisfy the lower passions of people; this is not true friendship for it takes no account of the respect that a person must have, both for himself and for the other as members of Christ's body. 'A man who does not love himself cannot possibly love another, for the love he offers his neighbour must be framed on the kind of love he has for himself.' It is evident he does not love himself if he commits base and immoral acts for himself. So truly Christian friendship never involves only two persons, Christ is always the third – and as soon as anything is said or done that would drive away Christ, then it ceases to be a Christian friendship. Aelred may be called the patron of friendship, but he will have nothing to do with friendship that uses other people simply to satisfy a personal need.

He speaks of the care with which one should choose one's friends, of how one should test them to see if they are worthy of confidence, because friendship involves a sharing of personal thoughts, an opening of the doors of heart and mind. This is something one cannot do fully with everyone and so friendship is of its nature 'particular'; it also involves a certain constancy and stability. A man does not change his friends, he says, as a child changes his toys. The great enemy of friendship is mistrust; though the loyalty which is its opposite does not mean that we should be blind to the faults and defects of our friends. It is here that true charity is needed; not simply to destroy the defect in our friend but to draw out and develop what is good in him. For that good was placed in him by God, and our love must always build up. Often we are at first drawn to others because of similar interests and ideals and then as we get to know them better we become aware of the differences between us. We realize that our friend is 'other', that he is not simply a reflection of ourselves. This is the time to adapt, to accept him as he is, as a person in his own right; and then the friendship becomes enriching on both sides.

Human friendship involves loyalty, generosity, patience, understanding and unselfishness – all elements of that charity which is the gift of the Holy Spirit, the Spirit of Jesus. So, if these things are practised, then there is a growth in that charity which is of God and a gradual transformation into the likeness of Jesus. Aelred points out that friends pray for each other; but the essence of prayer is not attention and preoccupation with what one is praying for, but a communion and being-with the person one is praying to. And thus in prayer a man passes from the love of his friend and from the union of wills that exists between them, to the presence and love of Christ. And thus, beginning with the love with which he embraces his friend and rising to the love with which he embraces Christ, he will come to that complete security where he will rejoice in the everlasting presence of the God of all goodness. Then this friendship to which on earth he can admit only a few, will be extended to all, and by all will be extended to God, since God will be All in all.

'The day before yesterday,' Aelred wrote, 'as I was walking round the cloisters, all the brethren sat together ... and in the whole of that throng I could not find one whom I did not love, and by whom I was not loved, and I was filled with such great joy ... that I felt my spirit was transfused into them and their affection was flowing back into me.' This does not mean that Aelred never felt strong emotion like anger, but he tells us that he never allowed the sun to set upon his anger. It does not mean that he did not have his critics – it was to answer some of these that Walter Daniel wrote his biography and the *Letter to Maurice*. It does not mean that his monks were never angry with him – one of them once picked him up as he lay in his cell and threw him on the embers of the fire. But it does mean that as he lay dying he could say 'God who knows all things knows that I love you all as myself, and as earnestly as a mother does her sons.' It was in his relationship with his community, and in the kind of monastery he wanted his abbey to be that we find the best expression of his character and spirituality.

Without question he had a great love for Rievaulx itself. He knew those days when the driving rain swept across the valley, leaving an icy cold in the stone buildings, but he also enjoyed those times when the warm sun was caught and trapped in the large cloister garth. He said he had always loved peace and inward quiet and he especially loved the quietness of the valley broken only by the sounds of the rooks nesting in the tall trees on the ridge, and the wood pigeons in the woods on the slopes, the bleating of the sheep, and in the spring the incessant cries of the young lambs; and then during the working hours the sounds of building – for much building was done while he was abbot – making a background of chip-chip as the masons cut and shaped the stone. But he made Rievaulx more than a place of outward quiet and peace; we are told that he 'turned the house into a stronghold for the sustaining of the weak, and the nourishment of the strong. Who was there, however despised and rejected who did not find in it a place of rest? Monks in need of compassion and mercy, men to whom

no other house gave entrance came to Rievaulx the mother of mercy, and found the gates wide open.' He would remind the brethren that it was the special and supreme glory of the house of Rievaulx that above all else it taught tolerance of the infirm, and 'compassion with others in their needs; it was a holy place because it brought forth for its God sons who were peacemakers.

Aelred was above all an Abba – a father to his community – and we find the quintessence of his life as Abbot spelled out in his 'Pastoral Prayer' addressed to our Lord, the Good Shepherd. He asks: 'What have I undertaken? Is not this your family, your special people, created and redeemed by you and gathered together from far and wide, souls dear to you put in my charge. Lord, since you have put me in this office or at least allowed others to put me here, you have an obligation to look after those entrusted to me.' Then, just as a priest is bound to offer sacrifice first for his own sins, he prays for his own needs. He asks God to look at his soul and to see him as he really is, and then to heal him like a good physician, correct him like a kind mother, forgive him as a forbearing father. He asks for his own needs, but also for what he needs for those entrusted to him. He wants to be a power for good rather than merely a superior. Solomon had asked for wisdom to rule his people; Aelred's people are 'those redeemed by the amazing love you showed on the Cross'. 'My God, you know what a fool I am – I ask for nothing, only that you would send me wisdom to be with me, work with me, act in me, speak in me, to order all my plans – do this for their advancement and my salvation.'

He prays for the good of all: 'Whatever you have given me, Lord, I want to give entirely to them – my work-time, my leisure, my activity and thinking, when things go well and when they go wrong, let all be spent on those for whom you deigned to spend yourself.' He asks for patience to bear with their shortcomings, sympathy to share their griefs, and the power to speak the truth plainly in a way that will be acceptable to the character and understanding of each.

He wishes the Holy Spirit to protect and shield them, to keep them united within themselves, with one another and with himself, to keep them chaste and humble, to cheer them up and help them in all the troubles of life. In their fasting, work, silence and repose 'let each one know that this Holy Spirit is with him in all his trials and temptations.' He asks for what they need in temporal matters, and that he may be a good steward distributing wisely and fairly whatever they have, be it much or little. And so may they persevere with gladness in their holy undertaking until they attain to everlasting life and the presence of their Lord and Helper.

It is a moving little document and taken together with his Sermons it shows his great perception and understanding of men, together with the insights he had in the subtle dangers and difficulties of community life. He saw more clearly than most men that if a community is a little mystical body then each has something different to contribute for the good of the whole, whether it be of work, prayer, artistic talents or simply gifts of character. This in itself meant accepting a certain form of plurality, and yet often members of a community expect all to be contributing the same things. He told those who were tempted to opt out from full community life, that to withold one's talents is a form of avarice, and is to defraud the community. The community must be close-knit like a coat of mail because through the weakness of one or two links the enemy could wound the whole body.

Throughout the last year of his life he was so weakened and wearied by his various infirmities that he would lie as if unconscious on his pallet – a tiny figure shrunken and dried up like a leaf of parchment. On the morning of Christmas Eve 1166, he spoke to the brethren in Chapter and told them of his longing to depart and be with Christ. He went to Vigils and preached in Chapter on Christmas Day, attended Mass and Vespers sitting near the presbytery steps not far from one of the great square Norman pillars in the church he loved so well. He was carried back to his cell where he lay exhausted, and as the days passed he grew weaker and weaker. On 3 January 1167 with all his monks around him he bade farewell and asked their prayers as he had done so many times before, when setting out on a journey. He made no will for he had nothing of his own – and he gave them back his psalter, the *Confessions of St Augustine* and his copy of St John's Gospel, together with the little cross which had belonged to Henry Murdac, and some relics of the saints. On 5 January he was anointed by Roger of Byland and the community came to see him, now twelve, now twenty, now forty, now a hundred gathered about him. He lingered on for three days more, murmuring from time to time: 'Hasten, for the love of Christ, hasten.' The day before he died Richard of Fountains, Roger of Byland and two other abbots with nearly all the monks were with him while one of them read the Passion. Walter Daniel held his head and whispered: 'Lord, gaze on the Cross: let your eye be where your heart is.' Aelred raised his eyes and said: 'You are my God and my Lord. You are my refuge and my Saviour. You are my glory and my hope for evermore. Into your hands I commend my spirit.'

But though he did not speak again and died about 10.30 p.m. on 12 January 1167, his spirit lives on. And today Cistercian monks have a deep desire to interpret for their own times the traditions and spirituality which Aelred and his contempories in the Order, first lived and then handed on.

Their vision persists that the Rule of St Benedict is a practical way of living out the Gospel and reflecting the hidden years of Our Lord's life at Nazareth and at prayer on the mountain side. The General Chapters of recent years have given guidelines for the observance of the Rule in the changed conditions of the modern world. So that without destroying the fundamental observances of the Rule, it can be expressed and lived in different cultures and cirumstances. A fervent community like that of Rievaulx under Aelred could act like a magnet drawing men to itself – giving an answer to the question 'What must I do to obtain eternal life?' But of course the real magnet is Christ himself, speaking not 2000 years ago or even 900 years ago, but now each day, in the hearts of those he draws to himself with the words 'Follow Me'. And the call does not simply come once, with a 'vocation' ten, twenty or thirty years ago, but it is constantly renewed ten, twenty or thirty seconds ago. Just as God calls afresh each day, so the monk's response can also be renewed times without number as he goes through the changing and unforseen circumstances of the journey through life. The prayer of the monk, whether in Aelred's day or in our own, is still that of the Psalmist: "Lord you are my portion and cup. There is one thing I ask of the Lord, for this I long, to live in the House of the Lord all the days of my life."

BIBLIOGRAPHY

Walter Daniel, *The Life of Aelred of Rievaulx* (trs. Powicke. introd. Dutton: Cistercian Fathers Series 57, Cistercian publications, Kalamazoo).

Paul Diemer, *Love without Measure*: extracts from the writings of Saint Bernard (Darton Longman and Todd, 1990).

D. Knowles, *The Monastic Order in England* (2nd edition, Cambridge 1963).

Louis Lekai, *The Cistercians: Ideals and Reality* (Kent University Press, 1977).

Aelred Squire o.p., *Aelred of Rievaulx, a Study* (Cistercian Studies Series 50, Cistercian Publications, Kalamazoo).

Aelred's works are printed in Latin in J.F. Migne, P.L. 195 and by C.H. Talbot in *Sermones Inediti* (1952).

Translations into English: *The Mirror Of Charity* (Cistercian Fathers 17). *Spiritual Friendship* (Cistercian Fathers 5). *Jesus at 12 yrs old, Rule for a Recluse, The Pastoral Prayer.* (Cistercian Fathers 2. Cistercian Publications, Kalamazoo). *Letter to his Sister* (G. Webb & Walker, 1955).

For futher information on the Cistercian life today, please contact Mt St Bernard Abbey, Coalville, Leics.

"O Good Jesus, let your voice sound in my ears, so that my heart and mind, and my inmost soul may learn to love you and the very depths of my heart may cling to you who are my delight and joy."

Abbot Aelred